Eating

Gill Tanner and Tim Wood

Photographs by Maggie Murray
Illustrations by Pat Tourret

A & C Black · London

Here are some of the people you will meet in this book.

The Hart family in 1990

Lee Hart is the same age as you.
His sister Kerry is eight years old.
What is Lee's mum called?

The Cook family in 1960

This is Lee's mum Linda when she was just nine years old in 1960. She is with her mum and dad, her brother and her baby sister.

The Smith family in 1930

This is Lee's granny June
when she was just a baby in 1930.
Her brother Jack is looking after her.

The Barker family in 1900

This is Lee's great grandma Lucy
when she was six years old in 1900.
Can you see what her sister
and her brothers are called?

How many differences can you spot
between these two photographs?

One shows a modern family eating a meal
and the other shows a family having tea
over one hundred years ago.

This book is about eating.

It will help you find out how
eating has changed
in the last hundred years.

There are twelve mystery objects in this book
and you can find out what they are.
They will tell you a lot about people in the past.

These mystery objects
belonged to the Barker family in 1900.
The objects are about the same size
as they appear on this page.
The object on the left is made of metal.
The other object is made of china.
You may have something like it at home.
What do you think they are?

Turn the page to find out.

Can you find the mystery objects in this picture?
It is Charles Barker's birthday.
The children have made him a special breakfast.
Fred is making toast on the fire with the toasting fork.
Harry has put a boiled egg in his own elephant **egg cup**
for his father.

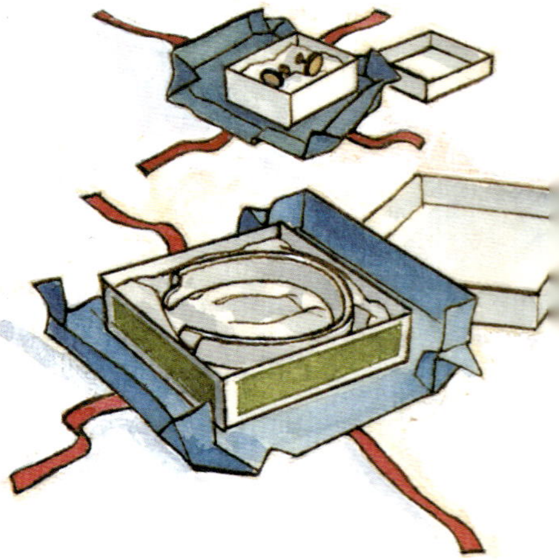

Charles Barker is using a pair of **egg scissors**
to cut the top off his egg.
He puts the metal loop over the top of the egg.
He closes the scissors to cut off the top.
Does your breakfast look like this?
How many differences can you spot?

The Barker family used this mystery object at tea time.
It is made of a metal called brass.
The object is in two parts.
The bigger part rests on a three-legged stand.
You may have something like it at home,
but yours may be made of stainless steel or plastic.

Can you guess what it is for?

Turn the page to find out.

Aunt Rose has come to visit the Barker family.
They are all in the parlour having tea.
Can you spot the mystery object in this picture?
It is a **table kettle**.

The burner under the kettle
keeps the water hot.
Alice pours hot water
from the kettle into the teapot.
Amy takes a cup of tea to Aunt Rose.
Lucy passes round the sandwiches.
Harry looks at the cakes
on the cake stand.
Do you eat your tea sitting at a table
with all your family?

These mystery objects are made of metal.
They are about the same size
as they appear on this page.
You can see that they are spoons.
But do you know what they were used for?
The two on the right both have holes in.
The two on the left are shaped like leaves.
Can you guess what they are?

Turn the page to find out if you are right.

The Barkers are at a garden party.
Can you see the mystery objects in the picture?
Alice is having a scone.
She uses a **jam spoon** to put jam on her scone.

Amy and Lucy are eating strawberries.
Amy is using a **sugar sifter**.
The sugar falls through the holes in the sifter
so it sprinkles evenly over the strawberries.
Do you have any special spoons in your home?

These mystery objects
belonged to the Smith family in 1930.
The object on the right is about the same length
as the bottom of this page.
It is a metal sieve with a wooden handle.
The object on the left is a metal box with a round lid.
Can you see what is in it?
What are these things called?

Turn the page to find out.

The Smith family are having breakfast.
Can you see the mystery objects in the picture?

Lucy Smith is making the tea.
She takes tea leaves from the **tea caddy**.
She puts them into the teapot
and pours boiling water on them.
When she pours out the tea she uses a **tea strainer**
to stop the tea leaves going into the cups.
Do you make tea like this?

The Smith family used these mystery objects when they went on picnics.
The grey objects are made of metal.
The brown objects are made of cardboard.
They all fit together in a clever way.
Can you guess what they are?
Can you work out how they fit together?

Turn the page to see if you are right.

Lucy and June are getting the picnic ready.
Richard and the other children are having a walk.
Richard gives Jack and May a drink of water.
He uses a water bottle and a set of **folding cups**.

Each cup is made of
three rings of different sizes.
When the three rings are fitted together
they make a cup for drinking.
The smallest ring has a base
which makes the bottom of the cup.
The rings can be put inside each other
to fit back into their cardboard box.

These mystery objects are made of metal.
They have bone handles.
You can probably see that they are knives and forks.
But do you know why they are shaped like this?
What were they used for?

Turn the page to find out.

The Smiths are eating their supper.
It is fish and chips.
Can you see the mystery objects in the picture?
They are **fish knives** and **fish forks**.

In those days people used
different knives and forks
for fish and meat.
Fish forks are smaller than normal forks.
Fish knives have wide blades
to make it easier to lift the fish off the bones.
Fish knives don't need to be
as sharp as meat knives.
Can you work out why?

These mystery objects belonged to Linda Cook in 1960.
She used them when she was on holiday.
They are made of metal.
You can probably see that they are a knife, fork and spoon.
But why do they have holes in the handles?

Turn the page to find out.

Linda is getting ready to go to a Brownie Pack camp.
Can you see the mystery objects in the picture?
June is packing Linda's rucksack.
Linda is putting her **travelling cutlery set** together.

She lines up the knife and fork on top of the spoon.
Then, she slides the handles so that the mushroom-shaped studs fit into the bottom of the keyhole shapes.
This locks the knife, fork and spoon together.
They are easier to carry this way and won't rattle in Linda's rucksack.

The Cook family used these mystery objects
when they ate out.
Each one is about the same size as a large orange.
They are made of plastic.
Do they remind you of anything?
Have you ever seen anything like them before?
What do you think they are?

Turn the page to find out.

The Cook family have just been to see a film.
Now they are in a burger bar having something to eat.
Can you see the mystery objects in the picture?
They are plastic **sauce bottles**.

The bottles are all shaped like tomatoes.
The green stalks unscrew so the bottles can be filled.
Each bottle is the same colour as the sauce inside it.
Andrew is putting tomato sauce on his chips.
David is putting brown sauce on his bun.
June is putting mustard on her burger.
What do you like on your chips?

Now that you know a bit more about eating
and how it has changed
over the last hundred years,
see if you can guess
what these mystery objects are.

They belonged to the Barker family in 1900.
The larger object is about the same size
as a page of this book.
The larger object is made of metal
and the smaller object
is made of wood and bristles.
You can probably see
that these are a dustpan and brush.
But can you guess
what they were used for at the table?

You will find the answer on page 24.

Time-Line

These pages show you the objects in this book and the objects which we use for eating nowadays.

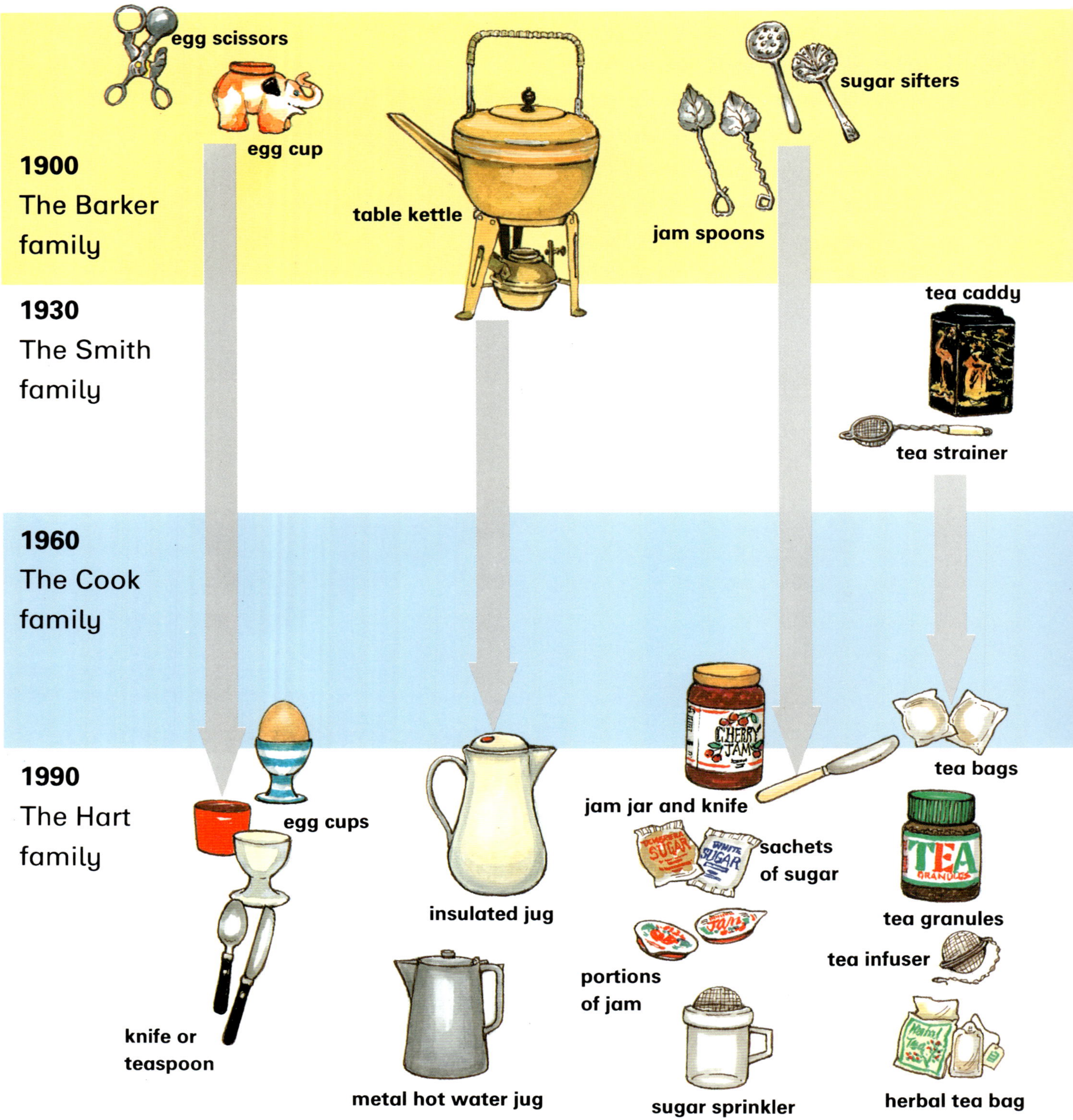

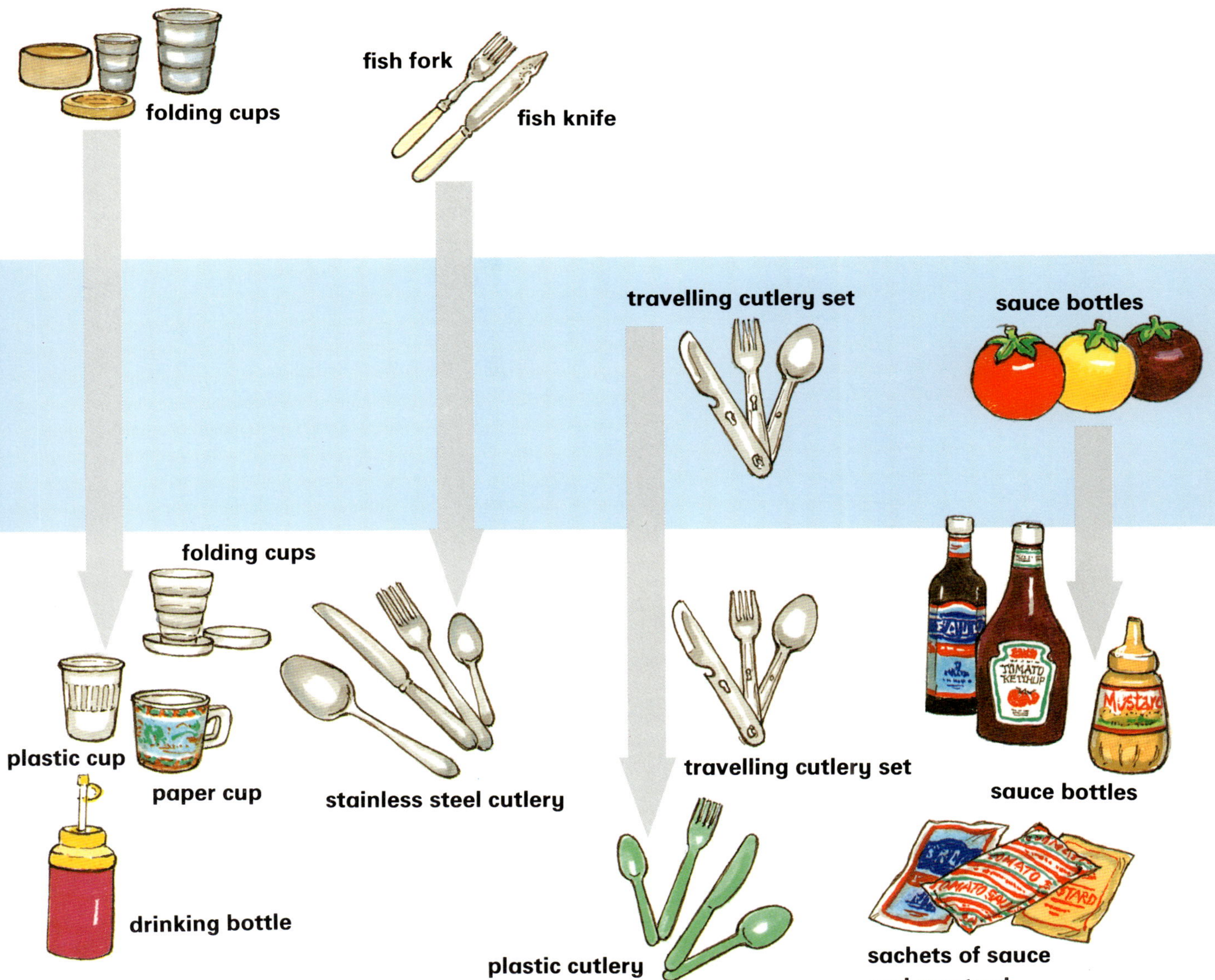
folding cups
fish fork
fish knife
travelling cutlery set
sauce bottles
folding cups
plastic cup
paper cup
stainless steel cutlery
travelling cutlery set
sauce bottles
drinking bottle
plastic cutlery
sachets of sauce and mustard

Index

The **mystery objects** on page 21 are a **crumb brush and tray**. At the end of the meal, after removing the crockery, they would be used to sweep up the crumbs on the tablecloth. This was much quicker and easier than cleaning the floor.

For parents and teachers

More about the objects and pictures in this book

Pages 5/6 The Victorians used many specialised eating and cooking implements, such as egg scissors. They are no longer used because of the decline of formal meals. In addition, most modern families wouldn't have the space to store these items nor time to clean them.

Pages 7/8 In Victorian and Edwardian times, meals were generally more elaborate and mealtimes lasted longer. This led to a whole range of items designed to keep food hot, or cooking, at the table. A small spirit lamp underneath the table kettle kept the water hot.

Pages 9/10 Before 1939, jam was sold in pottery jars which were too large for use at the table. Jam was served in china or glass dishes. Jam spoons were used to serve individual portions of jam.

Pages 11/12 Tea was first imported from China in 1609. It was very expensive. Tea was first sold in packets in 1826. The first tea bags for domestic use were produced by Tetleys and went on sale in 1952.

Pages 13/14 The folding cups used by the Smiths were made of aluminium. Tiny amounts of aluminium were first produced in 1825. The first aluminium cutlery was more valuable than gold. By 1888, aluminium could be produced very cheaply.

Pages 15/16 Fish knives do not need to be as sharp as meat knives because fish meat is soft.

Pages 17/18 Notice that the knife has a bottle-opener built into the handle. The travelling cutlery set is so practical that the design has hardly changed since the 1960s.

Pages 19/20 The sauce bottles were used in some of the first fast-food restaurant chains, such as Wimpy and Golden Egg. The bottles were made from brightly-coloured plastic, and were designed to look attractive and be fun to use.

Things to do

History Mysteries will provide an excellent starting point for all kinds of history work. There are lots of general ideas which can be drawn out of the pictures, particularly in relation to the way meals, family size and lifestyles have changed in the last 100 years. Below are some starting points and ideas for follow up activities.

1 Work on families and family trees can be developed from the families on pages 2/3, bearing in mind that many children do not come from two-parent, nuclear families. Why do the families in the book have different surnames even though they are related?

2 Find out more about meals in the past from a variety of sources, including interviews with older people in the community, books, museums, old postcards and photographs. Meals weren't the same for everyone. Why not?

3 There is one object which is in one picture of the 1900s, one picture of the 1930s, and one picture of the 1960s. Can you find it?

4 Arrange a field trip to a local museum or old house open to the public, where you can see what kitchens and dining rooms looked like in the past. This will tell you a lot about the elaborate preparations for, and presentation of, meals in the past.

5 Look at the difference between the photographs and the illustrations in this book. What different kinds of things can they tell you?

6 Make your own collection of pictures and objects to do with eating. You can build up an archive or school museum over several years by encouraging children to bring in old objects, collecting unwanted items from parents – such as old sauce bottles, packaging or cutlery – and collecting from junk shops and jumble sales. You may also be able to borrow handling collections from your local museum or library service.

7 Encouraging the children to look at the objects is a useful start, but they will get more out of this if you organise some practical activities which help to develop their powers of observation. These might include drawing the objects, describing an object to another child who must then pick out that object from the collection, or writing descriptions of the objects for labels or for catalogue cards.

8 Encourage the children to answer questions. What do the objects look and feel like? What are they made of? What makes them work? How old are they? How could you find out more about them? Do they do the job they are supposed to do?

9 What do the objects tell us about the people who used them? Children might do some writing, drawing or role play imagining themselves as the owners of different objects.

10 Children might find a mystery object in their house or school for the others to draw, write about and identify. Children can compare the objects in the book with objects in their own home or school.

11 If you have an exhibition, try pairing old objects with their nearest modern counterparts. Talk about each pair. Some useful questions might be: How can you tell which is older? Which objects have changed most over time? Why? What do you think of the older objects? What would people have thought of them when they were new? Can you test how well the objects work? Is the modern version better than the old version?

12 Make a time-line using your objects. You might find the time-line at the back of this book useful. You could include pictures in your time-line and other markers to help the children gain a sense of chronology. Use your time-line to bring out the elements of *change* (eg. the gradual disappearance of formal meals; the reduction in the number of eating implements; the increased popularity of convenience foods and snacks) and *continuity* (eg. the fact that we all need to eat; how meals are important for our health and as social events).

History Mysteries

First published 1995
A & C Black (Publishers) Limited
35 Bedford Row, London WC1R 4JH

ISBN 0-7136-4161-4

A CIP catalogue record for this book is available
from the British Library.

Acknowledgements

The authors and publishers would like to thank Jason King;
David Taylor; Mrs Tanner's Tangible History.

Photographs by Maggie Murray except for:
p.4 (top) Hulton Deutsch Collection; p.4 (bottom) Ulrike Preuss/
Format Photographers.

Filmset by Rowland Phototypesetting Limited, Bury St Edmunds, Suffolk
Printed and bound in the UK by Hunter & Foulis Limited, Edinburgh